BEHIND THE SCENES OF

LOST IN NEW YORK

Jordan Horowitz
Based on the screenplay written by John Hughes

SCHOLASTIC INC.
New York Toronto London Auckland Sydney

TWENTIETH CENTURY FOX PRESENTS A JOHN HUGHES PRODUCTION A CHRIS COLUMBUS FILM
MACAULAY CULKIN JOE PESCI DANIEL STERN HOME ALONE 2
FILM EDITOR RAJA GOSNELL PRODUCTION DESIGNER SANDY VENEZIANO DIRECTOR OF PHOTOGRAPHY JULIO MACAT EXECUTIVE PRODUCER MARK RADCLIFFE
DOLBY STEREO IN SELECTED THEATRES WRITTEN AND PRODUCED BY JOHN HUGHES DIRECTED BY CHRIS COLUMBUS COLOR BY DELUXE®
HUGHES
1991 TWENTIETH CENTURY FOX

These credits are tentative and subject to change.

ISBN 0-590-45720-9

Book designed by Ursula Herzog

12 11 10 9 8 7 6 5 4 3 2 1   2 3 4 5 6 7/9

Printed in the U.S.A.   08

First Scholastic printing, November 1992

What would you do if you were home alone?

What would you do if you suddenly found yourself home alone because your family went on vacation and forgot to take you with them?

You might make dinner out of ice cream and hot fudge . . . You might watch all the videos your parents never let you watch . . . You might even have to protect your house from robbers . . .

That is what a movie producer named John Hughes thought when he decided to make the movie *Home Alone.*

The wardrobe mistress helps Mack get into costume

The first *Home Alone* opened in movie theaters in 1990. Many people went to see it.

The movie was so popular that many children, teenagers, and grown-ups saw it more than once!

When a movie is that successful the producers often decide to make a second movie, called a *sequel*. They know that the people who saw *Home Alone* want to see what happened to the characters after the movie ended.

The makeup artist highlights Mack's cheeks

Recently, Mr. Hughes wrote a screenplay called *Home Alone 2: Lost in New York*. It tells the story of the second time Kevin McCallister is separated from his family.

Almost everyone who worked on the first *Home Alone* movie got together to work on the sequel.

This is the story of how that sequel was made.

Chris Columbus directs Daniel Stern and Joe Pesci

By now you must have a lot of questions about how a movie is made.

What does a producer do?
Who writes the script?
Who designs the costumes?
What does the director do?

To answer these complicated questions we have to start at the beginning.

In the beginning there must always be a *screenplay*.

```
201    CONTINUED:  (2)                                              201

       INT.  DUNCAN'S TOY CHEST.  FRONT WINDOW.  CU.  KEVIN

       Kevin peers into the store.  He takes a deep breath and steels
       himself for the challenge ahead.
                               KEVIN
                    This is it.  There's no turning back.
                    Another Christmas in the trenches.

       He looks to his hand...

202    INSERT:  KEVIN'S HAND.  NIGHT                                202

       He wraps a Plaza envelope around a paving stone with a rubber   (X)
       band and sets it down.  The envelope is marked in Kevin's       (X)
       handwriting -- TO: MR. DUNCAN (THE GUY WHO OWNS THE STORE).     (X)

203    INT. DUNCAN'S TOY CHEST.  FRONT WINDOW.  NIGHT                203

       Kevin bangs his fist on the window.

       INT.  STORE

       Harry and Marv look up in alarm, fists loaded with cash.

       THEIR POV

       Kevin waves.

       CU.  HARRY AND MARV

       Their jaws drop.
                               MARV
                    He's back.

       THEIR POV

       Kevin raises his camera and snaps a picture.  FLASH!

       INT.  STORE.  HARRY AND MARV

       Washed with FLASH LIGHT.

                               HARRY
                             (incredulous)
                    He took our picture.

                               MARV
                    How's my hair look?

                                               (CONTINUED)
```

A page from John Hughes's screenplay of Home Alone 2

There can't be a movie until there is a screenplay.

A screenplay is just what it sounds like. It is a *play* written for the *screen* — the movie screen, that is!

In a screenplay the first thing the writer has to do is tell what the characters say. On the page shown above, a writer thought up the line in which Kevin says, "Another Christmas in the trenches." The writer then shows what the characters do and how they move. The writer made Kevin bang his fist on the window. Next, the writer tells what the movie will look like when the audience sees it up on the screen. Directions like "their POV" mean you see the scene from Harry and Marv's "Point of View." You see what they see. In this example, you see Kevin!

Screenwriter and producer John Hughes

A *screenwriter* is a person who writes the screenplay. Mr. Hughes is an experienced screenwriter who likes to write movies for kids and their families. In just ten years he has made twenty films! *Home Alone 2: Lost in New York* will be his twenty-first!

Mr. Hughes began his career as a screenwriter by writing the scripts for the movies *National Lampoon's Vacation* and *National Lampoon's Class Reunion*.

Mr. Hughes has also produced films from his own scripts such as *Pretty in Pink, Some Kind of Wonderful*, and *The Great Outdoors*.

Mr. Hughes sometimes directs the films he writes and produces such as *Sixteen Candles* and *Planes, Trains and Automobiles*. His most recent films have been *Dutch* and *Curly Sue*.

Kevin is up to his old tricks

One of the hardest parts of writing a sequel to a popular film is trying to think of a new story.

In *Home Alone 2: Lost in New York*, Mr. Hughes came up with a very funny story that mixed the best of *Home Alone* with a whole new idea.

Lost in New York ... the greatest mistake of Kevin's life

THE STORY

It is Christmastime and, as usual, the McCallister family is rushing to get to the airport on time. This year they are going to Florida for the holidays. Kate and Peter McCallister want to be sure they don't forget Kevin again.

However, there is a mix-up at the airport and Kevin ends up on a different plane. When he gets off the plane he realizes that the rest of his family is in Florida, but he is in New York City!

The first thing Kevin does is check himself into the best hotel in the city. Then he goes on a shopping spree in New York's largest toy store, Duncan's Toy Chest. It's a dream come true. So far he is having the greatest Christmas of his life.

Merry Christmas, Kevin!

That is, until he runs into Marv and Harry, the two burglars who tried to rob his house the last time he was home alone. Marv and Harry have escaped from prison and are planning to rob Duncan's Toy Chest. When Kevin learns of their burglary plans, he comes up with a plan of his own.

Marv and Harry chase Kevin all through the city. Finally, Kevin leads the crooks to his uncle's brownstone. His uncle is out of town. So no one is home.

Now Kevin is on his own turf. Through a series of clever traps Kevin escapes from Marv and Harry again. The crooks chase him to Central Park. It looks like he's in big trouble. But with the help of his new friend the pigeon lady, Kevin traps the crooks for good.

When the excitement is over, Kevin misses his family. By this time his family has flown to New York to find the mischievous boy. The McCallisters wake up Christmas morning to a huge Christmas tree and lots of presents. The toy store owner has sent all these gifts to Kevin for catching the crooks. Kevin has done a good deed and it will be a Merry Christmas for everyone.

Director Chris Columbus with Tim Curry as the concierge

With the story and script completed, Mr. Hughes switched roles from writer to producer.

Producers have many different jobs on a film. They often think up the idea for the film. Then they must figure out how much it will cost to make the movie. Finally, they have to hire the kind of people that will help them make the film turn out just right.

One of the most important jobs the producer needs to fill is that of the *director*.

Chris Columbus yells action

It is the director's job to take the story from the screenplay and put it on the screen. The director does this by choosing camera people and other men and women who have special training, rehearsing the actors, and deciding what kind of *shot* to take with the camera.

Chris Columbus is a director who has made many funny and exciting family movies. He is a screenwriter as well. He directed *Adventures in Babysitting* and wrote and directed *Only the Lonely* (which Mr. Hughes produced). Mr. Columbus also directed *Home Alone.*

In order to make sure that *Home Alone 2: Lost in New York* had the same kind of feeling as the first movie, Mr. Hughes decided to hire Mr. Columbus to direct the sequel.

Perfect!

The word movie is a nickname. It stands for the term *motion picture*. Like the word screenplay, motion pictures are exactly what they sound like: they are pictures that move. Actually they are a series of pictures that are taken with a special camera. When the pictures, also called *film*, are run through a movie projector at your movie theater, the projector speeds up the film so it *looks* like the pictures move.

As director, the most important job Chris Columbus had was to make sure the pictures they took with the camera could be put together to tell the story in the screenplay.

To make sure the movie looked the way he wanted it to, Mr. Columbus hired an artist to draw out some of his ideas ahead of time. This is known as *storyboarding*. It helped Mr. Columbus see how his ideas worked before he filmed them with the camera.

Making it snow in New York City

Directors tell their ideas for a shot or a series of shots to an artist. The artist then draws them out on paper. It looks something like your favorite comic book. Comic books are another way of telling a story with pictures.

Once the storyboards are done the director has a kind of picture map to follow. This is very helpful for tough action or chase scenes — and there are several of those in the *Home Alone* movies!

Mack and Chris Columbus discuss a scene

Working together Mr. Hughes and Mr. Columbus hired different kinds of people to do the many jobs that would help them make *Home Alone 2: Lost in New York* exactly the way they pictured it.

One of the most important parts of making a sequel is getting the actors to play their same roles again.

For *Home Alone 2: Lost in New York* most of the actors from the first *Home Alone* movie wanted to play their parts again.

Macaulay Culkin

THE STARS

John Hughes knew there was something special about
Macaulay Culkin right away. When Macaulay was nine, John
Hughes chose him to act with John Candy in the 1989 film *Uncle
Buck*. When Mr. Hughes had to find an actor to play in his next
film, a comedy about a little boy who is left home alone, he didn't
have to think twice about who would play the part.

By now everyone has heard of Macaulay Culkin. Most people
know him by his nickname "Mack." At just 12 years old Mack is
the highest paid child actor in movie history. He is so popular
that people always want him to play parts in movies, television,
and TV commercials.

Mack and director Chris Columbus

Mack started acting when he was only four years old. He appeared in a play with his older brother Shane. People thought he was very good. After that he appeared in an *Afterschool Special.*

By the time he was seven Mack got his first big movie role. He played one of Burt Lancaster's grandchildren in the movie *Rocket Gibraltar.* That part led to other films such as *See You in the Morning* with Drew Barrymore and Lukas Haas, and *Uncle Buck* with John Candy.

Since the success of *Home Alone,* Mack has been a busy actor. He starred in his own Saturday morning cartoon series, appeared in a Michael Jackson video, and was even a guest host on *Saturday Night Live.* He did all this along with making movies!

Daniel Stern as Marv and Joe Pesci as Harry

The toughest roles in the *Home Alone* movies are those of Harry and Marv. They're the two crooks who always get caught in Kevin's traps.

In *Home Alone* Harry and Marv were hit in the head with a bucket, covered with glue and feathers, and forced to slide off icy steps.

In *Home Alone 2: Lost in New York* they get more of the same. They are covered with plaster, pelted with bricks, and attacked by a flock of pigeons!

Hiya pal!

Joe Pesci returns as Harry, the bungling mastermind crook.
Mr. Pesci also began acting when he was a child. He first
appeared in a 1950s television show called *Star Time Kids*.

He studied acting over the years and made many films in the
1970s. His role in Martin Scorcese's *Raging Bull* (starring
Robert DeNiro) made him famous. Since then he has appeared
in the *Lethal Weapon* movies and received an Academy Award
for his role in the movie *GoodFellas*.

The last film Mr. Pesci starred in was *My Cousin Vinny*.

Daniel Stern is back playing the role of Marv, Harry's dim-
witted partner-in-crime.

Mr. Stern remembers "making all the grown-ups laugh" when
he was a kid. He thinks this is what made him decide to become
an actor later in life.

He spent many years playing roles in the New York theater. He
got great reviews when he appeared in the movie *Breaking
Away*. Since then he has appeared in Barry Levinson's film
Diner and is the "voice" of the adult Kevin Arnold, the
narrator of ABC-TV's *The Wonder Years*. He has directed the
show many times.

John Heard

Catherine O'Hara

THE SUPPORTING CAST

Catherine O'Hara and John Heard are back, too. They play Kevin's forgetful parents, Peter and Kate.

Ms. O'Hara began acting in Toronto's Second City. This is the comedy group where John Candy and Rick Moranis also got their start. Since then she has appeared in such films as *Heartburn*, *After Hours*, and *Beetlejuice*.

As Kate McCallister, the mother of the five McCallister children, Ms. O'Hara is perfectly cast: after all, she herself has six brothers and sisters!

John Heard made his first film in 1977. He is a respected Broadway stage actor. Mr. Heard has been in many movies. Recently he was in the hit films *Big*, *Awakenings*, and *Radio Flyer*.

In *Home Alone 2: Lost in New York* Mr. Heard once again plays Peter McCallister, Kevin's father.

Marv gets a paint job

CHARACTER ACTORS

No sequel would be complete without offering something new. Apart from setting the story in New York City, the largest and most exciting city of them all, John Hughes has created several funny new characters.

Sometimes an actor can take a small role and make it stand out. The actors who play these parts are called *character actors*. Character actors play small but special roles. Mr. Hughes and Mr. Columbus cleverly cast a group of character actors to fill these new roles.

Eddie Bracken as Mr. Duncan with Mack

Dana Ivey, Tim Curry, and Rob Schneider

Dublin-born Brenda Fricker plays the pigeon lady, an unusual old woman who becomes Kevin's friend during his adventures in New York. Ms. Fricker has acted on television in England many times. She won an Academy Award for her role in the 1989 film *My Left Foot*.

Talented Tim Curry plays Mr. Hector, the concierge of the Plaza Hotel. This British actor leaped to fame when he appeared as Dr. Frank N. Furter in the movie *The Rocky Horror Picture Show* in 1975. He was in the original stage play of *Hair*. He has also been in many other films, including *Annie, Clue*, and the animated *FernGully: The Last RainForest* as the voice of Hexxus.

The part of the Plaza's frazzled bellman, Cedric, is played by Rob Schneider. Mr. Schneider is well-known for his character of Rich, the copyboy on NBC-TV's *Saturday Night Live*. He has also appeared in the big-screen comedies *Necessary Roughness* and *Martians, Go Home*.

Brenda Fricker as the pigeon lady

Dana Ivey plays the Plaza's front desk clerk. Ms. Ivey often acts in plays in New York. She has won awards for her work in *Driving Miss Daisy* and *Quartermaine's Terms*. She has been in the movies *The Color Purple, Dirty Rotten Scoundrels,* and last year's comedy smash *The Addams Family.*

The kindly toy store owner, Mr. Duncan, is played by Eddie Bracken. Mr. Bracken has been acting for more than sixty years! He began his career in the *Little Rascals* short films. He also starred in the Preston Sturges movies *Miracle of Morgan's Creek* (1944) and *Hail the Conquering Hero* (1944). In recent years he has been seen in *National Lampoon's Vacation* (written by John Hughes) and *Oscar.*

*To get a shot from high above,
they put the camera on a special crane*

Putting the camera on tracks helps it move smoothly

The script was written . . .
The director was chosen . . .
The actors were hired . . .
John Hughes and Chris Columbus were now ready for the next
phase of making *Home Alone 2: Lost in New York.*

In the following pages, you will learn about all of the other
talented men and women who helped make *Home Alone 2: Lost
in New York.* Each person had a different, but important job to
do to make the movie you saw in the theater.

The director uses an eyepiece to decide the best shot

Cinematographer Julio Macat looks through the lens, too

CINEMATOGRAPHY

Next to the director, the *cinematographer* is the most important person on the *set*. A set is the place where a movie scene is filmed. It is the cinematographer who makes the film look the way the director wants it to look.

First the cinematographer finds out where the director wants to put the camera for a shot. Then the cinematographer and the director look at the storyboards and decide what will be in the shot. One shot might show Kevin going into a phone booth. The next shot might show Kevin using his Talkboy.

Following this discussion the cinematographer and director decide what kind of lens to use on the camera. Some lenses show a whole scene, like the outside of Kevin's house. This is called a *long shot*. Some lenses show just details of the scene, like Marv's face when he gets covered with paint! This is called a *close-up*. There are even lenses for in-between shots.

Huge reflectors
bounce the lights just right

Julio Macat takes a reading with his light meter

Finally, the cinematographer talks to the *gaffer*. The gaffer is the person who is in charge of the electricians. The cinematographer then tells the gaffer where to put the huge and powerful lights that will light a set.

Cinematographers and gaffers often work together to get just the right amount of light and shadow in the shot. The cinematographer uses a light meter to decide how much light the shot needs. Then the cinematographer and the gaffer place several lights around the set and aim them to get the right amount of light for that scene. The camera can then take the picture. It's very much like the flash on your camera at home.

By using special tools the cinematographer and gaffer can control the light to create different moods. Some of these tools reflect light. They're actually called *reflectors*. Other tools hold the reflectors in place. These tools are called *goboes*. Still other tools, called *scrims*, are put over the lights like filters. They make the light seem softer. This process takes a long time, but it is very important. The cameras can't start shooting until the lighting is just right!

It takes a microphone on a long pole, known as a boom mike, to get the best sound

The slate records the scene being shot

While the cinematographer is lighting the set there may be time for the actors and crew to work on other things. The director might rehearse the scene with the actors while they wait. The producers might meet with the *unit production manager*. This is the person who tells the movie crew where they are shooting the movie and what time to arrive on the set. He or she also has to get the props and supplies for the movie. A prop is something the actors use in a movie. Kevin's Talkboy is a prop. So are the paint cans, wrenches, and bricks that land on Harry and Marv! YIKES!

Macaulay Culkin may even study for a test he has to take with his tutor. Even movie stars have to go to school. They just have to do it on the set! When school-age children work in movies, they still have to go to school. The movie producers had to hire a special teacher for Mack to teach the young actor regular school subjects, like math and history. The tutor traveled with the cast and crew while the movie was being shot.

*Videotape helps the
director make sure the
shot is picture perfect*

Mack plays director

On location: Wollman Skating Rink in Central Park

A New York college is cast as the Children's Hospital

Often the actors will spend some time with fans who have gathered around to watch a scene being shot *on location*. That's when a movie is shot outside of a studio — like on the streets of New York City!

In fact, many of *Home Alone 2: Lost in New York*'s outside scenes were shot on the streets of New York. Shooting began on December 9, 1991, in New York City. Wollman Skating Rink in Central Park, Radio City Music Hall, and the Christmas tree at Rockefeller Center were all chosen as locations.

The cast and crew of *Home Alone 2: Lost in New York* then went to Chicago. In Chicago they shot scenes at O'Hare International Airport. They rented an empty indoor tennis court where sets were built to look like a rock quarry in Central Park!

Finally the cast and crew flew to Los Angeles and filmed on the backlots of Universal Studios. This was where they built Uncle Rob's street and brownstone house.

When you saw the movie could you tell what was a real location and what was just a movie set?

Tim Curry in the concierge's costume

The characters have to wear costumes that make them look like the part they play.

It is the *costume designer*'s job to make the characters' clothes look right for the part. Costume designer Jay Hurley had to do this when he designed the costumes for *Home Alone 2: Lost in New York.*

For the concierge, bellboy, and other employees of the Plaza Hotel, Mr. Hurley designed costumes to look like the real uniforms. This was very important since many of the real people who work at the Plaza appeared in *Home Alone 2: Lost in New York.*

The pigeon lady's cape makes her look like a big bird

Perhaps Mr. Hurley's biggest job in *Home Alone 2: Lost in New York* was making the costume that the pigeon lady wore.

For the pigeon lady, Mr. Hurley designed a special cape that would make her look "birdlike." No wonder all those pigeons gathered around her!

Animal coordinator, Mark Harden, gives the pigeon lady her pigeons

Speaking of the pigeon lady, it was no small job to arrange all of her feathered friends and make them do what the director wanted. Whenever animals are used in movies, the producers must hire someone to bring in and train the kind of animal they need.

Mark Harden, the animal coordinator, has supplied and trained all different kinds of animals for many different films. *Home Alone 2: Lost in New York* was one of his biggest jobs.

"The funniest thing about using the pigeons in *Home Alone 2: Lost in New York*," says Mr. Harden, "is how smoothly everything went!"

Kevin and the pigeon lady and her pigeons

The movie had several scenes that included the pigeons. First there was the pigeon lady and her "friends." Then there was a scene where Kevin had to feed some pigeons. Finally, there was the scene where Harry and Marv are foiled by a flock of pigeons!

In order to get the movie just right, Mr. Harden had to bring in 550 pigeons! Fifty of them were specially trained as the pigeon lady's birds. These were the birds that you saw perched on the pigeon lady and flocking around her throughout the movie.

"Pigeons learn by repetition," says Mr. Harden. They are "herd" animals, so it was natural for them to stay together and not fly off the set.

One problem Mr. Harden had in working with his pigeons was the fact that pigeons don't fly at night. But the script called for several scenes where the pigeons had to fly around Central Park at night.

To solve this problem the producers had production designer Sandy Veneziano build a model of a Central Park rock quarry on an empty indoor tennis court in Chicago. They filmed the scenes during the day, but the set looked like it was night. The pigeons knew it was daytime outside so Mr. Harden had no trouble getting them to fly.

Which one is Mack?

Harry and Marv ... or is it?

Stunt doubles do the dirty work

Exterior of Duncan's Toy Chest

Inside the greatest toy store in the world

As you now know, the set is the place where the action takes place. A *production designer* is someone who makes the sets look the way the screenwriter has described them in the script. The production designer also has to make the sets fit the producer's idea of how those sets should look.

Sometimes building a set is easy. All the production designer has to do is build a set to look like a real building or place — like Central Park. Other times production designers must think up and design the set from their own ideas. Ms. Veneziano had to create the design for the outside of Duncan's Toy Chest without a real building to copy.

For Duncan's Toy Chest, Ms. Veneziano had to imagine what the best toy store in the world might look like. By the looks of it the design was a success.

What do you think?

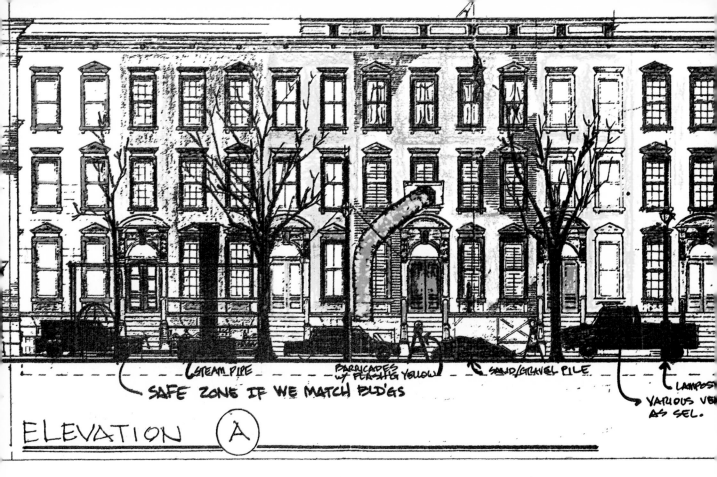

Original sketch of brownstone set design

A New York city street ... or is it? The actual brownstone set was built on an empty tennis court in Chicago and on a backlot at Universal Studios in California

Home Alone 2: Lost in New York began filming in early December, 1991, and ended in May, 1992. By the time they were done John Hughes and Chris Columbus had shot thousands and thousands of feet of film. Then came the job of taking all that film and putting it together to make a movie! This process is called *editing*.

To help him edit, or put the pieces of film together, Mr. Columbus hired Raja Gosnell, the *editor* who worked with him on *Adventures in Babysitting* and *Home Alone*.

When making a film the director often shoots the same scene many times in order to get it just right. The director also shoots the same scenes from many different angles, like looking up or down at the scene, or far away or close-up. This makes the scene look more interesting.

The editor is the person who takes all that film and, along with the director, chooses the best shots. Then, working at a huge editing machine, called a *moviola*, the editor *splices*, or joins the film together to make it look like one long story when you see it on a movie screen.

When all the editing is done the producers bring their film to special laboratories. The people in the laboratory put the movie's title or name on the film. They also list all of the people who helped make the movie. These lists are called *credits*. You see the credits at the beginning and end of the film. Another laboratory makes many *prints*, or copies, of the film. These prints will then be sent to movie theaters around the country.

The job of putting all these steps together could not have been done without the help of executive producers Mark Radcliffe (*Planes, Train and Automobiles, Home Alone*), Duncan Henderson (*Dying Young*) and Richard Vane (*Dutch, Harry and the Hendersons*). Their experience as film producers helped Mr. Hughes and Mr. Columbus make certain that production went along without any trouble.

Many films have more than one sequel. Now that you've seen *Home Alone* and *Home Alone 2: Lost in New York*, would you want to see another *Home Alone* film? What do you think could happen to Kevin McCallister next? Will Kate and Peter leave home without Kevin again? Will Marv and Harry escape from prison again?

You'll just have to wait and see . . .